THE
CUCUMBER
Cookbook
25 Delicious Recipes with Cucumber:
Salads, Soups, Appetizers, Snacks,
Smoothies, Drinks and Exotic Meals

Contents

Your Gift
I wanted to show my appreciation that you support my work so I've put together a free gift for you.

http://bonusfreebook.org/

Just visit the link above to download it now.

Introduction

You know what summertime means for us veggie geeks, a whole load of wholesome cucumbers! They are among the easiest vegetables to use in the kitchen because they are extremely cool, versatile and crispy.
What is more? Cucumbers are a great source of essential vitamins C, K and potassium.
When you are in your local grocery store willing to buy some cucumbers, you should know about some tricks. Choose a smaller size, cucumbers that are smooth and colored evenly.
I would also recommend checking the tips since older cucumbers tend to go soft at the tip - steer. As for the varieties, that is up to you. Organic ones are not bitter at all, so you can consider leaving the peel while cooking.
You can pair your cucumbers with anything you like, to come up with delicious salads appetizers, snacks, soups and smoothies. This is because cucumbers have a neutral flavor, which will sit back and allow all the other ingredients to bring out their flavor.
If you love cucumbers as much as I do, here is a list of easy and remarkable recipes that are worth giving a try.

CHAPTER ONE

-

Salads

Salads are an all-time favorite for a wide majority of people, for not only those looking to shed off some pounds, but those of us who prefer light meals every day.

Cucumber salads are very easy to make, because most of them are eaten raw so you will not spend any time in the kitchen cooking. All you need is to prepare the ingredients and voila, there will be your salad.

The salads are light, healthy, very delicious and watery, hence perfect for a hot summer day. You will never go wrong with cucumber salad.

Cauliflower Corn and Cucumber Salad

Cucumber is such a great addition to your regular cauliflower salad because it makes the otherwise heavy dish become very light and delicious. You can make this delicious salad ahead of time and refrigerate until you decide to serve it. You can also enjoy this as an addition to your favorite casserole.

Preparation time: 15 minutes
Serves: 2

Ingredients:

Small cucumbers, diced – 2
Cauliflower florets, chopped – 2 cups
Red pepper, diced – ½
Green onions, sliced – 3
Canned corn, well drained – 15 oz.
Mayonnaise – ½ cup
Fresh dill, chopped - ½ cup
Salt and pepper according to your taste

Method:

Add all your veggies into a large salad bowl and mix well.
Stir in the mayo, salt, pepper and fresh dill.
Toss to make sure all the ingredients are well combined.
Serve chilled.
Enjoy!

Honeydew Cucumber Salad

You will love this salad because it is a mixture of vegetables and fruits, and not just your regular cucumber salad. Moreover, it is vegan, gluten free and paleo. You can enjoy this for lunch or breakfast, or even when out for a picnic. It also makes a great side dish for shrimps, barbecue or steak.

Preparation time: 10 minutes
Serves: 1

Ingredients:

Honeydew melon – 1
Cucumber, peeled and chopped – 1
Red onion, sliced – ½
Fresh dill, chopped – 2 tablespoons
For the dressing:
Lemon juice, freshly squeezed – 2 teaspoons
Olive oil – ¼ cup
Honey, pure – 1 teaspoon
Salt and black pepper according to your taste

Method:

Add all your salad dressing into a small bowl and mix until well incorporated. Set aside.
Meanwhile, cut your melon and remove the seeds and rind.
Cut into small chunks and add into a large salad bowl
Add your cucumber, onion and dill.
Drizzle your salad dressing and toss to combine all the ingredients.
Store in the refrigerator until you are ready to serve
Enjoy!

Cucumber Feta Salad

Do you love cheese? Well, this is a very simple way you can incorporate it in your salads. This salad has a Greek flare that you will definitely like even more because of the lemon-balsamic dressing. Additionally, it is healthy and very easy to make.

Preparation time: 20 minutes
Serves: 2

Ingredients:

English cucumbers, sliced into rings – 2
Red onion, thinly sliced – 1
Bell pepper, cut into strips – 1
Feta cheese – ½ cup
For the balsamic dressing:
Olive oil, extra virgin – 2 tablespoons
Vinegar, balsamic - 1 tablespoon
Lemon juice, freshly squeezed- 2 tablespoons
Salt and black pepper according to your taste

Method:

Mix your dressing ingredients in a small bowl until all the salt dissolves.
Add your salad ingredients into a salad bowl except for the cheese
Drizzle your dressing and toss to mix
Sprinkle a generous amount of feta cheese to the salad and combine well
Serve immediately!

German Cucumber Salad

Are you looking for an exotic salad to spice things up in your kitchen? Look for it no more. Our German cucumber salad is extremely easy to make with very few ingredients that you already have at home. The traditional salad calls for sour cream, but we used yogurt instead.

Preparation time: 20 minutes
Serves: 2

Ingredients:

Cucumber, peeled and sliced – 1
Yogurt, plain – ½ cup
Large tomato, diced – 1
Onion, thinly sliced – 1
Lemon juice, freshly squeezed – 4 tablespoons
Fresh dill, chopped – 1 tablespoon
Kosher salt according to your taste

Method:

In a large salad bowl, combine the dill and salt
Add your plain yogurt and lemon juice, whisk to mix everything well
Stir in the remaining ingredients and toss to coat them well with the dressing
Serve and enjoy!

Cucumber Caprese Salad

This is your traditional cucumber caprese salad but with a twist. We love this salad because it has loads of vegetables that are very nutritious. What is more? You can enjoy the salad as your main dish, or pair it up with turkey legs, barbecue chicken, burgers or steak.

Preparation time: 30 minutes
Serves: 2

Ingredients:

Peeled cucumber, skin scraped with fork and thinly sliced – 1
Cherry tomatoes, quartered – 1 ½ cups
Fresh mozzarella, shredded – 8 oz.
Large red onion, thinly sliced – ½
For the dressing:
Olive oil, extra virgin – 2 tablespoons
Vinegar, balsamic – 1 tablespoon
Oregano, dried – 1 tablespoon
Basil, dried – 1 tablespoon
Kosher salt and black pepper according to your taste

Method:

Mix your dressing ingredients in a small bowl. Set aside.
In a medium-sized bowl, add the rest of your ingredients and toss to mix well.
Pour your dressing over the salad and mix to coat the vegetables.
Allow the salad to sit for about 10 minutes before serving.
Enjoy!

CHAPTER TWO

-

Appetizers, Snacks and Sides

When you have many cucumbers at home, there are a lot of dishes you can make with these fantastic vegetables. Preparing delicious appetizers, snacks or sides to your barbecue meat or pastry is another way to go.

We love cucumber snacks because they allow us to substitute the starch we regularly use, that has lots of sugar and other additives. Cucumbers have a neutral flavor, which gives you a chance to fully experience the magic in the flavor of other ingredients you will use.

The recipes below make perfect snacks that can be enjoyed even at parties, or as an appetizer before you have the main meal. They are very simple recipes, which involve no cooking.

Cucumber Bruschetta

This cucumber salad is a fun twist added to your regular cucumber and tomato salad. The fresh crispy cucumbers combined with juicy tomatoes and a hint of garlic will have you scrapping whatever is in your dish. It also makes a perfect topping for your toasted baguette.

Preparation time: 20 minutes
Serves: 4

Ingredients:

English cucumber, diced – 1
Tomato, diced – 1
Garlic clove, well minced – 1
Fresh basil, chopped – 3 tablespoons
Olive oil, extra virgin - 1 tablespoon
Vinegar, red wine – 2 teaspoons
Kosher salt and black pepper according to your taste
To serve:
Baguette – 1
Olive oil, extra virgin
Garlic clove – 1

Method:

Toss all your ingredients together in a medium mixing bowl.
Combine to incorporate them well.
Slice your baguette into ¾-inch slices.
Brush the top of each slice with some olive oil.
Broil in the oven for about 2-3 minutes or until your baguette is lightly toasted.
Remove the toasted slices from the oven and rub each with the fresh garlic clove
Spoon the cucumber salad over the bread.
Serve and enjoy!

Lemony Cucumber and Cream Cheese Sandwich

We all have those lazy days when a sandwich is the only thing we are able to make for a light lunch or a snack. You will love the tangy flavor from the lemons, and the creamy texture brought on by the cheese. These sandwiches will be your absolute favorite in no time.

Preparation time: 10 minutes
Serves: 12

Ingredients:

Large cucumber, seeded and thinly sliced – ½
Cream cheese, softened – 4 oz.
Fresh dill, chopped – 2 tablespoons
Lemon juice , freshly squeezed – ½ lemon
Lemon zest – 2 tablespoons
Salted butter, softened – 4 oz.
Kosher salt – 1 teaspoon
Black pepper, freshly ground – ½ teaspoon
Grain bread, white or whole – 6 slices

Method:

Combine cheese, dill, lemon juice and zest in a small bowl and season with salt and pepper.

Gently spread your salted butter on each slice

Lay your slices on a work surface, with the buttered sides facing up

Distribute your cream cheese mixture on each slice evenly

Dry your cucumber slices using a paper towel and arrange them on the first 3 slices

Top the 3 slices with the ones remaining without the cucumber

Slice crusts off the slices and serve immediately, each sandwich is sliced into 4 triangles. If they are not ready to serve, wrap your sandwiches tightly with a cling film and store in the refrigerator for about 24 hours.

Enjoy!

Dilly Cucumber Bites

If you have plenty of fresh cucumbers and wonder just what to do with them, here is an idea for you. Our dilly cucumber bites are super amazing, very simple to make and turn out to be the best cucumber appetizers you will ever have. It is made of all veggies so the bites are also very healthy. If you do not have a piping bag, just snip off one corner on a zip lock bag and you are good to go.

Preparation time: 15 minutes
Serves: 4

Ingredients:

Big English cucumbers, thinly sliced into rounds – 4
Grape tomatoes, quartered – 1 pint
Block cream cheese, room temperature – 8 oz.
Greek yogurt, plain – 5.3 oz.
Fresh dill, well minced – 3 tablespoons
Ranch dressing mix, powdered – 1 teaspoon

Method:

Place your cucumber rounds on a serving tray
Combine your cream cheese, yogurt, and minced dill, ranch the dressing in a small bowl
Mix well to incorporate all the ingredients together until you get a smooth creamy mixture
Transfer this mixture to a piping bag.
Pipe your cheese mixture onto all the cucumber slices
Top each slice with half of the cherry tomato
Enjoy!

Cucumber Avocado Rolls

These cucumber avocado rolls are light snacks that you can enjoy with your family or serve at parties. Not only do they look good, they taste even better. What is more? They are so simple to make and do not require many ingredients.

Preparation time: 20 minutes
Serves: 10

Ingredients:

Cucumber , peeled – 1
Ripe avocado, diced – 1
Fresh basil leaves, chopped – ¼ cup
Garlic clove, well minced – 1
Lime juice, freshly squeezed – 2 teaspoons
Salt – ¼ teaspoon
Yeast, nutritional – 1 tablespoon
Black pepper, freshly ground – 1 teaspoon
Paprika for garnish

Method:

Add all your ingredients except for the cucumbers and paprika into a food processor or blender.

Pulse on high until you obtain a smooth but creamy mixture.

Slice your cucumbers into long thin stripes. You can use a mandolin or potato peeler for this.

Spread a thin coat of the avocado mixture along the length of each cucumber strip

Roll your strips up.

Sprinkle a little paprika on each cucumber roll.

Serve immediately.

Enjoy!

Cucumber Hummus Cups

These cucumber and hummus cups are made for a really interesting and delicious summer snack or appetizer. They are very simple to prepare, you do not even need any cooking and they taste so heavenly.

Preparation time: 15 minutes
Serves: 8

Ingredients:

Large cucumbers, – 4
Hummus – 1 cup
For the hummus:
Roasted garlic – 1 tablespoon
Low sodium chickpeas, well rinsed and drained – 1 can
Olive oil – 1 tablespoon
Lemon juice, freshly squeezed – 2 tablespoons
Water – 2 tablespoons
Salt – ½ teaspoon

Method:

Cut off the ends of your cucumbers.

Slice each into about ¼-inch slices.

Using a spoon, scoop out seeds from each slice, making sure you leave a thin layer at the bottom to hold the hummus.

Place your cucumber slices, scoop side down on a paper towel to dry out all the moisture for about 15 minutes.

Meanwhile, prepare the hummus by adding all the ingredients into a blender or food processor and blending on high speed until you get a smooth creamy consistency

Keep refrigerated, in an airtight container, until you are ready to use them. You can keep for up to 5 days

Spoon about 1 teaspoon of your hummus into each cucumber cup.

Serve immediately and enjoy.

Baked Cucumber Chips

These cucumber chips are considered perfect and healthy snacks, if you are trying to steer away from the regular store bought chips that have loads of calories. They are vegan, gluten-free.

If you love chips and still want to maintain a healthy lifestyle, get those cucumber slices and bake them. The best part is that you can customize the flavors just the way you like it.

Preparation time: 4 hours
Serves: 5

Ingredients:

Large cucumbers, thinly sliced into rounds – 2
Lemon juice, freshly squeezed – 1 teaspoon
Black pepper, freshly ground – ½ teaspoon

Method:

Start by lining your baking sheet with a parchment paper and set aside.

Pat your cucumber slices dry using a paper towel to get rid of the excess moisture.

Add your slices to a large bowl and mix with your lime juice and black pepper

Arrange your seasoned cucumber slices on the lined baking sheet

Proceed to bake at 170 degrees F for about 3-4 hours.

When they are dried out and crispy, remove your slices from the oven.

Serve and enjoy

CHAPTER THREE

-

Soups

Cucumber soups are so popular especially in summer because cucumbers tend to have high water content and it is just what you need to keep you hydrated and refreshed.

Instead of having the regular cold drinks, filled with sugar and other additives, try out our chilled cucumber soups and you will never look back. They are extremely easy to make and you need just a few ingredients like watermelons and tomatoes that are abundant in summer.

Beet and Cucumber Soup

The beetroot has numerous health benefits that you would not really want to miss out. Coupled up with cucumbers, it is made for a delicious and refreshing soup bound to keep you going all summer.

Preparation time: 10 minutes
Serves: 2

Ingredients:

Cucumbers, seeded and diced – ½ cup
Peeled beets, cubed and boiled – 2
Chicken stock – 1 cup
Greek yogurt, plain – ½ cup
Lemon juice, freshly squeezed – 1 tablespoon
Sugar – 2 tablespoons
Kosher salt and freshly ground black pepper to taste
Sour cream and fresh dill for garnish

Method:

Add all your ingredients into a blender, apart from the garnish and seasoning.
Blend on high speed until you obtain a smooth puree.
Season with salt and pepper as you like.
Transfer the soup into a bowl and chill for at least 4 hours or overnight, while covered with a plastic wrap
When you are ready to serve it, add a dollop of sour cream and some fresh dill
Enjoy!

Watermelon and Cucumber Gazpacho

If you are looking for a refreshing summer drink bursting with vibrant flavors, our cucumber gazpacho is the perfect soup for you. It is a gluten-free and vegan cold soup with loads of veggies and fruit that will keep you hydrated on hot days.

Preparation time: 2 hours
Serves: 4

Ingredients:

English cucumber, chopped – 1
Watermelon, chopped – 4 cups
Cherry tomatoes, diced – 1 pint
Red onion, thinly sliced – ½
Lime juice, freshly squeezed – ¼ cup
Fresh basil, chopped – ½ cup
Salt – ½ teaspoon
Black pepper- ¼ teaspoon

Method:

Reserve about ¼ of your veggies after chopping to add to the soup later on.
Add the remaining ingredients into a blender and pulse on high speed until all the ingredients are well combined.
Transfer your soup into a bowl.
Stir in your reserved ingredients.
Refrigerate for about 1-2 hours.
Serve chilled and enjoy.

Cucumber Avocado Soup

For a low-carb chilled drink which is healthy and filled with flavor, our cucumber and avocado soup fits the bill perfectly. Especially if it is the avocado season, you cannot do without this soup because it is simply worth it; there is no cooking involved, and it is so easy to prepare.

Preparation time: 20 minutes
Serves: 6

Ingredients:

Cucumber, peeled and chopped – 16 oz.
Ripe avocados, pitted and halved – 2
Red onion, thinly sliced – 2 tablespoons
Sour cream – ½ cup
Lime juice, freshly squeezed – 4 tablespoons
Jalapeno pepper, seeded and chopped – 1
Chili powder – ½ teaspoon
Fresh cilantro, chopped – 2 tablespoons
Sea salt – ½ teaspoon

Method:

Reserve some cilantro and about 3 tablespoons of the cucumber.
Add the remaining ingredients into a food processor or blender
Blend until you get a thick and creamy consistency.
Transfer the soup into an airtight container and store in the refrigerator until you are ready to serve.
Serve garnished with the reserved cilantro and cucumber.
Enjoy!

Cucumber and Buttermilk Soup

Even when you are in need of a cold soup on a hot day, who says it cannot be super thick and creamy? Our cucumber and buttermilk soup is best made ahead of time to allow all the flavors to blend in together. It is tasty, and it can also be enjoyed as dessert after a lovely meal.

Preparation time: 1 hour
Serves: 6

Ingredients:

Small thin cucumbers, peeled and chopped – 4
Buttermilk – 3 cups
Sour cream – ¾ cup
Olive oil – 2 teaspoons
Kosher salt – ½ teaspoon
Garlic clove, well minced – 1
For the garnish:
Diced tomatoes
Fresh chives, chopped
Kosher salt and black pepper
Olive oil
Cucumber, finely diced

Method:

Set aside about ¼ of your diced cucumbers for the garnish.

Add the rest of your ingredients into a blender and pulse for about 2 minutes or until the mixture is smooth.

Pour your soup into a bowl and store in the refrigerator for at least 1 hour or until chilled.

For an extra chilled soup, store in the freezer for about 15 minutes before serving.

Serve topped with your preferred garnish ingredients and some olive oil.

Enjoy!

CHAPTER FOUR

-

Smoothies and Drinks

Cucumbers can be used for quite refreshing smoothies and drinks due to their very high water content. Moreover, they have a neutral flavor and therefore they will not alter the desired taste of your drinks.

You can enjoy your smoothies either as a breakfast option or a snack. They are very nutritious and are much better than filling up on sweet snacks that will only expand your waistline. Cucumber smoothies are also a perfect post workout drink.

They also come in handy when making your adult beverages, be it margaritas, sangrias, coolers or mojito. You do not have to go all the way to the bar for a cocktail anymore. And your friends will surely thank you for the amazing cocktails every weekend.

Strawberry, Banana and Cucumber Smoothie

If you are looking for a gluten-free and vegan smoothie that you can enjoy for breakfast, as a snack or after your workouts. Our strawberry, cucumber and banana smoothie is just a perfect fit. Cucumber brings in the spa-like feel to the smoothie, with its overrefreshing properties that will keep you hydrated all day. Feel free to use your favorite greens if you do not like spinach much. You can also substitute chia seeds with flax seeds.

Preparation time: 10 minutes
Serves: 1

Ingredients:

Cucumber, peeled and chopped – 1
Strawberries, frozen – 1 ½ cups
Ripe banana, sliced and frozen – 1 ½
Almond milk, unsweetened – 1 cup
Chia seeds – ½ tablespoon
Spinach, chopped -1/2 cup

Method

Start by defrosting your strawberries to get them soft.

Add the milk and cucumber slices into a blender and pulse on high speed until you get a smooth mixture.

Add in your strawberries, bananas, chia seeds and spinach and keep blending on high until you obtain a creamy but smooth consistency.

Keep adding a bit of almond milk until you attain your desired level of thickness.

Serve immediately!

Enjoy!

Mango, Cucumber Mint Smoothie

This is quite a refreshing drink, healthy and very nutritious. It has no added sugar since it gets its sweetness from the mango. This smoothie is a perfect summer blast that you can enjoy any time of the day or after dinner. Have we also mentioned that it is upper low in calories?

Preparation time: 10 minutes
Serves: 2

Ingredients:

Cucumber, peeled and diced – 2 cups
Frozen mango, cubed – 3 cups
Milk – ½ cup
Lime juice, freshly squeezed – 1
Mint leaves, fresh – 3

Method

Add all your ingredients into a blender.
Blend until you get a smooth puree.
Enjoy!

Pineapple, Coconut and Cucumber Smoothie

You will love how the coconut and pineapple flavors blend to create such an amazing smoothie, which is creamy and it tastes great. Cucumbers have a neutral flavor but they have numerous health benefits that make your smoothie perfect even as a post-workout drink or the one for breakfast. You can use either spinach or kale for your greens.

Preparation time: 10 minutes
Serves: 3

Ingredients:

Organic cucumber, skin on and sliced – 1 ½ cups
Pineapples, cubed – 3 cups
Frozen banana, sliced – 1 ½
Coconut milk, light – ¾ cups
Water, filtered – 1 ½ cups
Organic greens – 210 g
Hemp seeds - 2 tablespoons
Ice cubes - 8

Method:

Add all your ingredients into a blender.
Mix on high speed to obtain a creamy and smooth consistency. If you need a thicker smoothie, use more ice, and for a thinner one, add more liquids.
Serve immediately
*Leftovers can be kept in the refrigerator for up to 24 hours.
Enjoy!

Watermelon and Cucumber Mojito

Whenever you are craving for an adult drink on a Friday night, why not trying this very simple mojito recipe? It is quite refreshing and very tasty and just the perfect cocktail to get your mind at ease.

Preparation time: 20 minutes
Serves: 4

Ingredients:

Seedless watermelon, pureed – 1
English cucumber, pureed – ½
Limes, freshly squeezed -2
Mint, muddled – 1 cup
Vodka, chilled – 8 oz.
Large sparkling water, chilled – 1
Ice cubes

Strain your pureed watermelon and cucumber using a sieve to remove all the pulp. Set your juice aside.

Put your limes and mint into a bowl, muddle using a wooden spoon.

Add your mixture into a shaker with the ice and shake for around 20 seconds

Strain into a large pitcher.

Add your watermelon and cucumber juice to the pitcher.

Pour in your vodka and the sparkling water.

Serve in cocktail glasses and enjoy.

Spicy Cucumber Margaritas

Are you too lazy to go out to the bar for your favorite margarita? You can easily whip some all by yourself, and even manage to make the drinks extra spicy, just the way you like it. Happy hour has never been so exciting.

Preparation time: 20 minutes
Serves: 2

Ingredients:

Cucumber, sliced- 1
Tequila – 4 oz.
Lime juice, freshly squeezed – 2 oz.
Orange juice, freshly squeezed – 1 oz.
Agave – 1 tablespoon
Jalapeno, thinly sliced – 1
Extra thin cucumber slices, jalapeno slices and lime wedges for garnish
Ice cubes
For the sweet chili rim salt:
Chili powder – 1 tablespoon
Kosher salt, coarse – 1 tablespoon
Sugar – 1 tablespoon

Add your cucumber slices, tequila, lime juice, agave and orange juice into your blender.

Pulse for about 1 minute or until you get a smooth puree.

Strain out your liquid and add into a cocktail shaker.

Stir in your jalapeno slices and muddle in the margarita until you achieve your desired level of heat

Add some ice cubes and shake the mixture for about 1 minute. Set aside

Meanwhile, whisk all your rim ingredients in a small bowl.

Run a lime wedge around the edge of your cocktail glasses.

Dip the glasses into salt until the rim is well coated.

Strain your margarita into your cocktail glasses.

Add more ice cubes and top with the extra garnishes if you like.

Enjoy!

For all the gin lovers out there, here is a delightful recipe that you can enjoy at the summertime. It is a very light and refreshing cocktail that you can enjoy even after dinner. The choice between basil or mint leaves for the cocktail remains entirely up to you. They both taste great.

Preparation time: 10 minutes
Serves: 2

Ingredients:

Cucumber, peeled and pureed – 2
Gin – 2 shots
St. Germain liqueur – 1 shot
Lime juice, freshly squeezed
Club soda - 4 shots
Simple syrup – 1 shot
Ice cubes
For the simple syrup
Water – 1 cup
Sugar – 1 cup
A handful of basil or mint leaves

Method:

Strain your cucumber puree through a fine mesh strainer to completely remove the pulp. Set your juice aside.

To make the simple syrup, heat your sugar solution and bring to boil.

Reduce the heat to low and add a handful of basil or mint leaves and allow to simmer for about 3 minutes.

Remove the mixture from heat and strain out the leaves.

Store your syrup in the refrigerator.

Add the gin, liqueur and the rest of the ingredients into a cocktail shaker.

Shake vigorously and strain your mixture over your cocktail glasses with rocks.

Top with club soda and serve!

CHAPTER FIVE

-

Exotic Dishes

It is about time you ditch your traditional cucumber recipes and try the exotic dishes that you have not known about before.

These are not your regular salads that you make every day. They are all exotic recipes, specifically based on a certain country's delicacies. This is one way you can surely impress your guests, using your knowledge of food cooked around the world.

Here is a rundown of a few simple recipes that you may fancy trying.

If you have been filing up on lots of meat lately and are finally looking for awesome meatless dishes, how about trying this exotic cucumber one? It is fresh, healthy, crunchy and full of flavors. It is a simple easy to make dish; you will definitely enjoy it. Baby romaine or Boston lettuce will be the perfect leaves for the salad.

Preparation time: 25 minutes
Serves: 5

Ingredients:

Cucumber, diced – ¾ cup
Tomatoes, chopped – ¾ cup
Cooked Quinoa, chilled – 2 ¼ cups
Fresh parsley, chopped – ½ cup
Green onions, sliced – 3
Fresh mint, finely chopped – 1 tablespoon
Cumin, ground – ½ teaspoon
Garlic salt – ½ teaspoon
Lemon juice, freshly squeezed – 3 tablespoons
Olive oil, extra virgin – 3 tablespoons
Feta cheese, crumbled – 1/3 cup
Kosher salt and pepper according to your taste
Lettuce leaves

Method:

In a medium-sized bowl, mix all your ingredients together, save for the cheese.

Fold in your crumbled cheese and season with salt and pepper

Chill your salad for about 30 minutes.

Spoon the salad on your lettuce leaves.

Serve immediately and enjoy!

Cucumber Pasta with Indonesian Peanut Sauce

Many Indonesian dishes always come with a pretty generous serving of peanut sauce, popularly known as bumbu kacang. Cucumber pasta is quite a delight because it is watered down due to the high content found in cucumbers, making it a light dish. When combined with the creamy sauce, you get a delicious dish, totally raw, vegan, wheat and gluten-free.

Preparation time: 30 minutes
Serves: 4

Ingredients:

For the pasta:
Large cucumbers, peeled– 2
Large carrot, peeled – 1
Cabbage, shredded -1 cup
Fresh cilantro- ¼ cup
Red onion, well minced – 1 tablespoon
Red bell pepper, chopped – 1 cup
For the peanut sauce:
Organic Peanut butter, raw – ¼ cup
Lemon juice, freshly squeezed – ¼ cup
Water – ¼ cup
Garlic cloves, well minced – 2
Fresh ginger, peeled and minced – ½ inch
Salt – 1 teaspoon
Hot cherry pepper, seedless – ½
Dates – 4

Start by spiralizing your cucumbers and carrot
Add into a large salad bowl alongside the rest of the ingredients
Mix well and set aside.
Put all your peanut sauce ingredients into a blender.
Pulse on high speed until you obtain a smooth puree.
Pour the sauce into a small bowl or drizzle over your salad.
Serve and enjoy!

Spicy Thai Cucumber Salad

This is a very interesting salad, with a classic Asian flavor, with just the right touch of sweetness and a hint of spiciness. If you love Thai food, then you will definitely enjoy this salad. It is perfect when enjoyed on its own, but you can also serve this salad as a side to a steak.

Preparation time: 30 minutes
Serves: 5

Ingredients:

Cucumbers, seedless – 2
Large carrots, cut into thin strips – 2
Green onions, sliced – 3
Peanuts, chopped – ¼ cup
For the dressing:
Vinegar, rice – 1/3 cup
Oil, sesame - 1 teaspoon
Red pepper flakes – ½ teaspoon
Sugar – 2 tablespoons
Salt – ½ teaspoon

Method:

Start by spiralizing the cucumbers.

Add the spiralized cucumbers alongside all other salad ingredients into a large salad bowl.

Mix until everything is well combined.

Add your salad ingredients into a small bowl and whisk until well incorporated.

Pour your dressing over the vegetables and toss to combine.

Garnish with extra peanuts and onion.

Serve immediately!

Enjoy!

Mexican Cucumber Fruit Salad

The trick to this Mexican fruit salad is the tangy and spicy lime dressing made to perfection. You can use all your favorite fruit for this and the result will be a vibrant salad that you will enjoy immensely. If you cannot find jicama in your local grocery, use green apples or pears as a substitute.

Preparation time: 20 minutes
Serves: 4

Ingredients:

English cucumber, well diced – 1 cup
Lime juice, freshly squeezed – 1 cup
Agave – 3 tablespoons
Ancho chili powder – ½ teaspoon
Cayenne pepper – 2 teaspoons
Kosher salt – ½ teaspoon
Seedless watermelon, diced – 1 cup
Jicama, diced – ½ cup
Pineapple, diced – 1 cup
Ripe mango, diced – 1 cup

Method:

Add your lime juice, agave, chili powder, cayenne pepper and salt into a small pot.

Heat on the medium heat for about 5 minutes, stirring constantly.

When it boils, remove the pot from the heat and set your dressing aside to cool.

Meanwhile, dice all your fruit in approximate one inch cubes each and store them separately in the refrigerator for about 5 minutes.

Serve immediately in smaller salad bowls and drizzle your dressing over the fruit.

Enjoy!

Conclusion

Cucumbers are awesome, and by trying the recipes, you might have realized that too.
You can pair them up with just about anything, be it fruit or veggies and the result will be an amazing super delicious food that you will enjoy. If you have not tried any of our recipes yet, it is a good time to start.
Happy cooking!

Your Gift
I wanted to show my appreciation that you support my work so I've put together a free gift for you.

http://bonusfreebook.org/

Just visit the link above to download it now.

Legal & Disclaimer
The information contained in this book and its contents are not designed to take a form of medical or professional advice; and are not meant to replace the need for independent medical, financial, legal or other professional advice or services, as it may be required. The contents and information of this book have been provided for the purposes of education and entertainment only.
The contents and information contained in this book were compiled from sources deemed reliable, and they reflect the best of the Author's knowledge, information, and belief. However, the Author cannot guarantee its accuracy and validity and cannot be held liable for any errors and/or omissions. Further, changes are periodically made to this book when it is needed. Whenever it is appropriate and/or necessary, you must consult a professional (including but not limited to your doctor, attorney, financial advisor or such other professional advisor) before using any of the suggested recommendations, techniques, or information in this book.

Before reading the contents and information contained in this book, you should agree not to hold the Author responsible for any damages, costs, and expenses, including any legal fees potentially resulting from the application of any of the information provided by this book. This disclaimer applies to any loss, damage or injury caused by the use and application, whether directly or indirectly, of any advice or information presented, whether it is the breach of a contract, tort, negligence, personal injury, criminal intent, or any other cause of action. You should agree to accept all risks of using the information presented in this book.

You should agree that by continuing to read this book, when appropriate and/or necessary, you shall consult a professional (including but not limited to your doctor, attorney, or financial advisor or such other advisor as needed) before using any of the suggested recommendations, techniques, or information in this book.